COLOR ME
Creative

An Adult Coloring Book for the Creative Muse In Everyone

Maya Sheppard

DEDICATIONS

First and always, to my mom who encouraged me to be a writer, even though she had no idea what I was writing about. She was a steadfast believer that I could do and be anything I wanted with joy, creativity, hard work and prayer.

To my father who would love me to be an accountant, but grudgingly respects my desire to be a world-class writer. His support is unwavering, and his loyalty to me and my creative efforts is without question.

And, last but certainly not least, to my daughter who is my enthusiastic partner in all writing endeavors. She has believed in me when I didn't believe in myself.

Every writer should be lucky to have a stellar lineup of supporters like this.

With God all things are possible.

PRAISE FOR COLOR ME CREATIVE

"This book helps with one of banes of a writer's life, staring at a blank screen wondering how to get started, and tap into that all elusive Muse. This handy resource combines adult coloring with writer's prompts, positive motivation, character building help and writer's resources guaranteed to help.

This book is for writers and non-writers alike. It is a fun, explorative journey that will bring out the creative side of anyone. Even if you're not a writer, you will love this book. And, if you are a writer, this book may be the creative kickstarter you've been looking for."

- Ruth Price, best-selling author of Out of Darkness

Why You Want This Book!

Writers face many challenges when creating, writing or getting started with their short stories and novels. By combining adult coloring, which is a meditative process, with writing prompts, jump starter writing exercises, inspirational quotes and much more, this writer's activity book is a great resource to beat writer's block, get new ideas and use adult coloring as a method to feed your creative Muse.

However, this book is not just for fiction writers.

It's also for people who non-fiction writers, as well as people who journal, blog poster creators, musicians writing lyrics and anybody else who loves to color.

Color Me Creative Will Get Anybody's Creative Jucies Flowing

It teaches how to let go and allow your Muse to run wild and free. It's meditative and for adult colorers, the designs are wonderful with an inspirational quote on the reverse side.

So, if you need inspiration, a way to relieve stress, have fun and meditate, Color Me Creative is the book for you. It's a unique resource that feeds your Muse, helps you unwind and lifts you up all at the same time.

Enjoy!

The aim of art is to represent not the outward appearance of things,
but their inward significance.
- Aristotle

He who is not courageous enough to take risks will accomplish nothing in life.
- Muhammad Ali

Take A Leap Of Faith

Writers are artists. Our creativity comes from taking leaps of faith using our imagination and simply going with the flow. No matter how much we plan, plot and outline, in the end we must fill empty computer screens and notebooks with worlds for readers to visit.

Agnes de Mille said it best:

"The artist never entirely knows. We guess. We may be wrong, but we take leap after leap in the dark."

What leap of faith did you take today?

_____

_____

_____

_____

"There is no passion to found playing small - in settling for a life that is less than the one you are capable of living."

- Nelson Mandela

Are you playing small with your writing?

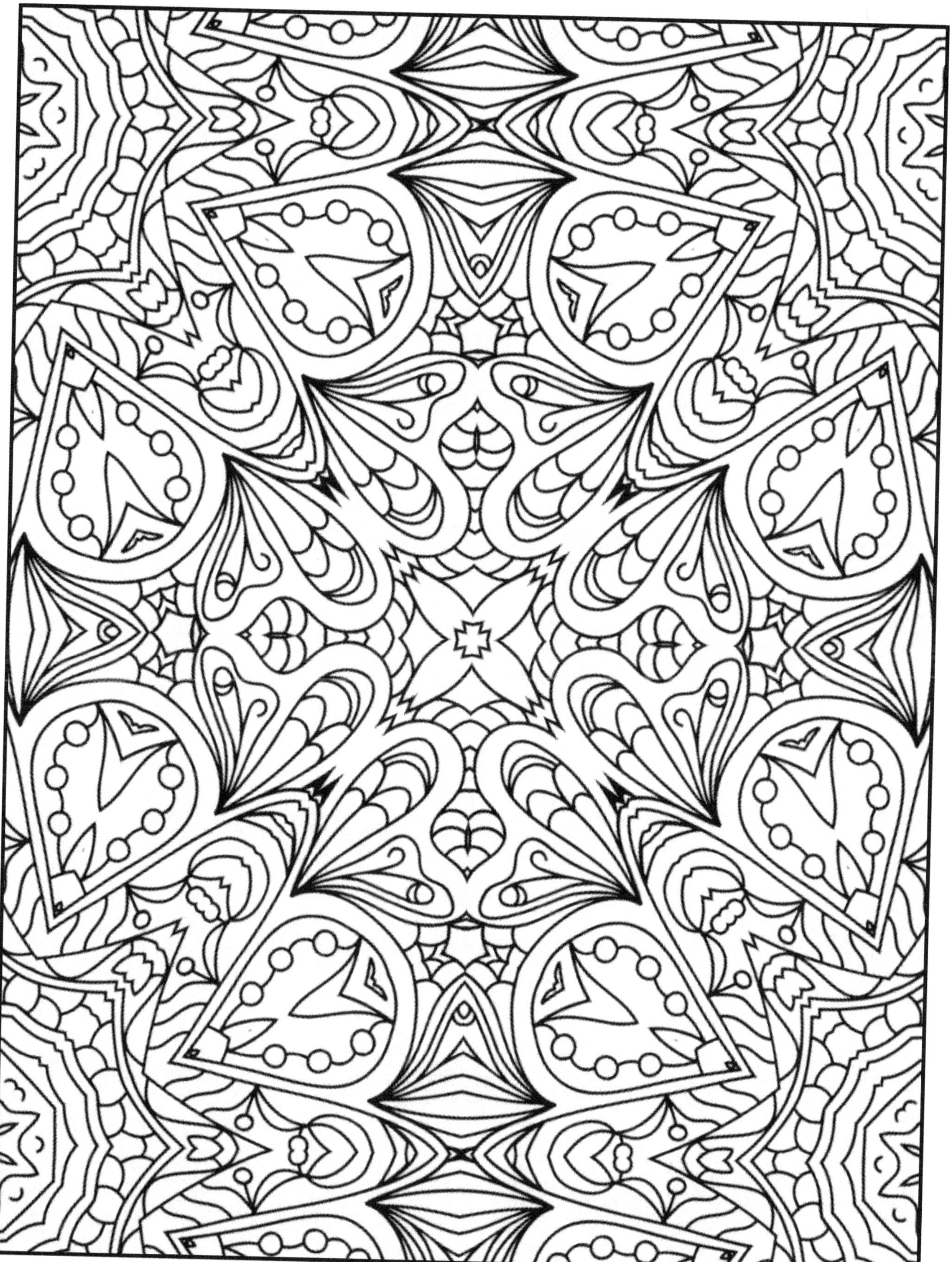

I like living. I have sometimes been wildly, despairingly, acutely miserable, racked with sorrow, but through it all I still know quite certainly that just to be alive is a grand thing.
- Agatha Christie

WRITE
WRITE
WRITE
NOW

Color This In & Send It To A Writer Who Needs A Writer's Block BREAKER,
even if that writer is YOU!

Nothing exists except atoms and empty space; everything else is opinion.
- Democritus

Writing Exercise

Writing is creative. One way to get the creative juices rolling is to take three or four disparate pieces of information and use them in a short, short story. Take the three pieces of information below and write a vignette using all three of them.

The only rule in this exercise is to write non-stop for 10 minutes. During that period, you will most likely hit a wall, where you think you've run out of things to write.

DON'T STOP. Keep writing even if all you can write is garbage, garbage, garbage, I have nothing else to write.

Here's the best part. When you keep writing past the wall, something magical will happen. You will hear a whisper; you will feel the next words starting to flow. Listen for it. Once you break through that wall, you will be in the zone, and you will write more and faster than you ever thought possible. Scenes will come to you quickly, and you just need to keep going until it stops.

Here are the three pieces of information:

1. The smell of bbq on the grill
2. A spiral staircase
3. The color blue

Turn the page and get started, or go straight to your computer and start.

Write for 10 Minutes

The smell of BBQ on the grill
A spiral staircase
The color blue

It's none of their
business that you have
to learn to write. Let
them think you were
born that way.
- Ernest Hemingway

And as imagination bodies forth

The forms of things unknown, the poet's pen

Turns them to shapes and gives to airy nothing

A local habitation and a name.

– William Shakespeare (from A Midsummer Night's Dream)

got
Story?

If you can tell stories, create characters, devise incidents, and have sincerity and passion, it doesn't matter a damn how you write.

– Somerset Maugham

To produce a
mighty book,
you must choose
a mighty theme.
- Herman Melville -

Develop an attitude of gratitude, and give thanks
for everything that happens to you,
knowing that every step forward is a step toward achieving
something bigger and better than your current situation.
- Brian Tracy

Characters Are A Writer's Best Friend

Writing a story is more about the characters than the plot. Now, I might get some blowback on that idea, but bear with me. Plot and structure is very important; there is no doubt about that. However, without characters to populate the story, it remains just a great outline.

So, with that in mind, let's write out a character.

First of all, you must have a clear vision of what your character is like. You must take the time to develop a character that is believable in whatever universe you're working in. Characters have certain characteristics no matter if they're in a detective novel or a science fiction novel.

When I plot out a character manually, I use the free EPIGUIDE located at EPIGUIDE.COM. It provides a FREE comprehensive character building chart that you can use to make your character have depth, idiosyncracies, principles and philosphies that make them believable within the context of the story.

On the next few pages, I have included the chart for you to use. It was something I used until I moved to software-driven character development.

The EPIGUIDE.COM Character Chart for Fiction Writers
This chart can be found at http://www.epiguide.com/ep101/writing/charchart.html

Character's Full Name: _____   Date: _____

Name origin: _____

Nickname, if any (if so, explain its origin – e.g. who created it?): _____

Does s/he like the nickname? _____

Birth date: _____

Place of birth: _____

Ethnic background: _____

Religion: _____

Degree of religious practice (e.g. orthodox, casual, lapsed):: _____

Current address: _____

Does s/he rent or own? _____

Brief description of home (apartment, house, etc.): _____

Does s/he live with anyone? _____

Describe the area in which s/he lives (city, town, rural, other): _____

Is this his/her ideal home and location? If not, what would s/he prefer? _____

Home decor: ☐ Expensive   ☐ Inexpensive   ☐ Carefully planned   ☐ Comfortable   ☐ Neat   ☐ Cluttered

Does s/he drive? Own a car? (Make, model, color, age, etc.): _____

Pets? (If so, what kind/how many/names?) _____

If so, how important are they? How well are they treated? _____

Current occupation (include length of time, location, job title): _____

Job satisfaction (happy, discontent, ambivalent, ambitious...): _____

Income: _____

Sexuality (e.g. straight, gay, bisexual, asexual, uncertain...): _____

Marital status: _____

If married or currently romantically involved, with whom, and for how long? _____

List any significant previous romantic partners:

_____

For current spouse/partner, what does the character call him/her (pet names, nicknames, etc.)?

_____

How did they meet?

_____

Any children (include names, ages, other parent if different from any current partner):

_____

_____

Describe his/her relationship with children (if any)?

_____

PHYSICAL APPEARANCE:

_____

Height: Weight: Body type (thin, athletic, overweight, curvy, muscular, etc.)

_____

Eye color: Need glasses/contacts/hearing aid?   Skin tone (pale, ivory, tan, olive, ruddy, brown, etc.):

_____

Face shape (round, oval, chubby, thin, long, square, heart-shaped, etc.:

_____

Any prominent features, freckles/moles/scars/tattoos or other distinguishing marks:

_____

Whom does s/he most look like (e.g. famous person or relative)?

_____

General health (good, excellent, poor...)?

_____

Any current health problems or chronic conditions?

_____

How does s/he dress?

Price: ☐ Expensive   ☐ Average   ☐ Inexpensive   ☐ Cheap

Style: ☐ Haute Couture ☐ Conservative   ☐ Trendy   ☐ Eclectic   ☐ Business   ☐ Sexy   ☐ Gaudy   ☐ Casual   ☐ Sloppy

Why does she dress in the above manner (e.g. to be noticed)?

_____

Any special jewelry? (If so, why is it special?)   What about accessories?

_____

Grooming: ☐ Fastidious/Very neat ☐ Average ☐ Clean but scruffy ☐ Dirty/Unkempt

If other than average, why?
_____

Describe hairstyle (long, short, crewcut, locs, bangs, side-part etc.):
_____

Natural hair texture (smooth, wavy, curly, etc.):   Current hair texture (if different):
_____

Natural hair color: Current hair color (if different):
_____

SPEECH AND LANGUAGE/COMMUNICATION:

Pace of speech (fast, average, slow?):   Voice tone (shrill, high, average, deep, squeaky, hoarse, harsh, authoritative, cultured, etc.):
_____

Accent/dialect, if any: Any favorite/habitual words/phrases? Curse words?
_____

Describe general vocabulary or speech pattern (e.g. educated, precise, pretentious, average, uneducated, vulgar...
_____

Mannerisms/demeanor?

☐ Cool/confident ☐ Volatile ☐ Nervous/shy ☐ Aggressive ☐ Friendly ☐ Remote ☐ Other (describe)
_____

Typical posture:

☐ Stiff ☐ Stands straight but not stiffly ☐ Average, varies with mood ☐ Slumped/defeated ☐ Slouchy, careless

☐ Relaxed ☐ Other (describe)

Gestures: ☐ Rarely ☐ Controlled ☐ When excited ☐ Most of the time ☐ Wildly/oddly ☐ Other (describe)
_____

Common/habitual gestures (e.g. nail-biting, hair patting, drumming fingers, clenched fists, hands in pockets, etc.)
_____

EVERYDAY BEHAVIOR / HABITS:

Finances: (prudent/cautious, some debt, lives paycheck to paycheck, deep in debt, criminal activity, etc.):
_____

Personal Habits: Smoking, Drinking, Drugs, Gambling, etc.? Are any of these addictions?
_____

Morning Routine: Describe the character's morning rituals. Who else is sleeping in the same bed? What time does he/she wake up? Is he/she cheerful in the morning? What does he/she do during breakfast-read, watch tv, feed kids, etc.

_____

Afternoon/Workday: Does s/he work outside the home? How does he/she get there? Is s/he good at this job? What if anything would he/she rather be doing? How long and hard is the work day? If the job isn't outside the home, what does a typical afternoon consist of?

_____

Dinner: Does s/he eat at home or go out a lot? What is/are his or her favorite restaurant(s)? Who cooks at home? Does s/he eat alone?

_____

Evening: What does your character do on a typical evening? Where? With whom? How much does he/she enjoy it? What is the ideal evening for him or her?

_____

Sleep Habits: Fall asleep easily, or an insomniac? Any recurring dreams? Sleep soundly, or toss & turn?

_____

Any special talents? Skills?

_____

What is s/he particularly *unskilled* at?

_____

Any hobbies (sports, games, arts, collecting, etc.)?

_____

FAMILY OF ORIGIN:

_____

Mother's name (include maiden name if known/applicable):

_____

Current status: __ living __ deceased (If alive, enter age: _____)

Mother's occupation, if any:

_____

Describe the mother's relationship with character:

_____

Father's name:

_____

Current status: __ living __ deceased (If alive, enter age: _____)

Father's occupation, if any:

_____

Describe the father's relationship with character:

_____

Any step-parents, foster parents, or birth parents (if not same as above):

(If s/he is adopted, does s/he know? If not, why?)

_____

Sibling(s) (include age and birth order relative to main character):

_____

Relationship(s) with character:

_____

Nieces/Nephews: In-Laws, if any:

_____

Other than the above, who else in the story is part of his/her extended family (e.g. cousins, etc.)?

_____

THE PAST:

Home town (if different from current home):
_____

Was his/her childhood happy? Troubled? Dull? Does the character remember it accurately?

_____

Earliest memory:
_____

Happiest memory:
_____

Saddest memory:
_____

How much school did s/he attend, if any? Did/does s/he like school? Why or why not?

_____

Most significant childhood event:
_____

Other significant childhood events:
_____

Significant past jobs:
_____

Police record (explain any convictions, sentence served, where/when):

_____

First crush/romantic love?
_____

What was his/her first sexual experience? Is it a positive or negative memory?

_____

Major illnesses, accidents or traumas? How is s/he still affected, if at all?

RELATIONSHIPS WITH OTHERS:

Who is his/her best friend? _____

Who are his/her other close friends? _____

How in general does the character relate to friends? _____

... to strangers? _____

... to spouse/Lover? _____

... to past spouses/lovers? _____

... to own children, if any? _____

... to other family members? _____

... to the same sex? _____

... to the opposite sex? _____

... to children in general? _____

... to others who are more successful? _____

... to others who are less successful? _____

... to boss (if any)? _____

... to underlings at work? _____

... to competitors? _____

... to authority (police, IRS, politicians, attorneys, doctors, etc.)? _____

What do most people consider his/her most likeable trait? _____

What do most people consider his/her biggest flaw? _____

Any secret attractions/crushes? _____

In romantic relationships, is s/he generally monogamous or uncommitted? (If the latter, is s/he honest w/ partners?)
_____

Is his/her sexual behavior inhibited, average, experimental, or reckless? Has this changed (and if so, why)?
_____

Whom does s/he dislike most, and why? _____

Whom does s/he like most, and why? _____

Who's the most important person in his/her life right now, and why?
_____

Whom does s/he secretly admire (nonromantic), and why? _____

Who was his/her biggest influence, and why? _____

Person s/he most misunderstands or misjudges: _____

Person who most misunderstands or misjudges him or her: _____

Has s/he lost touch with anyone significant in his/her life? If so, why? _____

Worst end of a relationship (could be friend, romance, colleague...)?

Whom does s/he most rely on for practical advice?

Whom does s/he most rely on for emotional support?

Whom, if anyone, does *s/he* support (e.g. advice or emotional support)?

MENTAL ATTITUDE/PERSONAL BELIEFS:

Any psychological issues (e.g. phobias, depression, paranoia, narcissism, etc.)?

Is s/he an optimist or pessimist?

Meyers Briggs Personality Type (see http://www.humanmetrics.com/cgi-win/jtypes2.asp):

S/he is most comfortable when ... (alone, hanging w/friends, drinking, etc.):

S/he is most uncomfortable when ... (in a crowd, alone, speaking in public, etc.):

Is s/he cautious, brave, or reckless in his/her approach to life?

What does s/he most value/prioritize (family, money, success, religion, etc.)?

Whom does s/he really love best?

Whom or what would s/he be willing to die for?

Is s/he generally compassionate or self-involved?

Personal philosophy:

What's his/her most embarrassing moment?

What is his/her secret wish?

What (or who) is his/her biggest fear?

Any prejudices (race, culture, sexuality, religion, etc.)?

Political party or beliefs, if any:

Does s/he believe in fate or destiny? Is s/he superstitious?

Character's greatest strength:

Other good characteristics:

Character's greatest flaw:

Other character flaws:

What are his/her own favorite attributes (both physical and personal)?

What about least favorite?

Are these feelings accurate?

How does s/he think others perceive him or her? (And is this accurate?)

Biggest regret:

Other regrets:

Proudest accomplishment:

Other accomplishments:

Quirks:

Character's biggest secret(s)? Who else knows (if anyone)?

How does s/he react to a crisis?

What usually causes the problems in his/her life (romance, finances, friends, rivals, colleagues, personality flaws, health, etc.)?

What would s/he most like to change about her-/himself? Why?

Write a paragraph (~100 words) of the character describing him/herself:

Short term goals:

Long term goals:

Does s/he plan to achieve these goals,
or does s/he think they're unrealistic?

Will others be affected? If so, does s/he care?

What if anything is stopping him/her from achieving these goals?

What event or occurrence does s/he most dread or fear?

What does he/she actively work to gain, keep or protect?

Which person in his/her life would s/he most want to emulate?

Which person in his/her life would s/he *least* want to emulate?

LIKES/FAVORITES:

Food:

Book:

Music/Song:

Motto/Quote:

Drink:

Film:

Sport:

Possession:

Color:

TV Show:

Hangout(s):

Character Notes & Doodles

Poetry creates the myth, the prose writer draws its portrait.
– Jean-Paul Sartre

Writing a novel is like driving a car at night. You can only see as far as your headlights, but you can make the whole trip that way.
– E. L. Doctorow

First, find
out what your
hero wants, then
just follow him!
- Ray Bradbury -

I have been successful probably because I have always realized that I knew nothing about writing and have merely tried to tell an interesting story entertainingly.

– Edgar Rice Burroughs

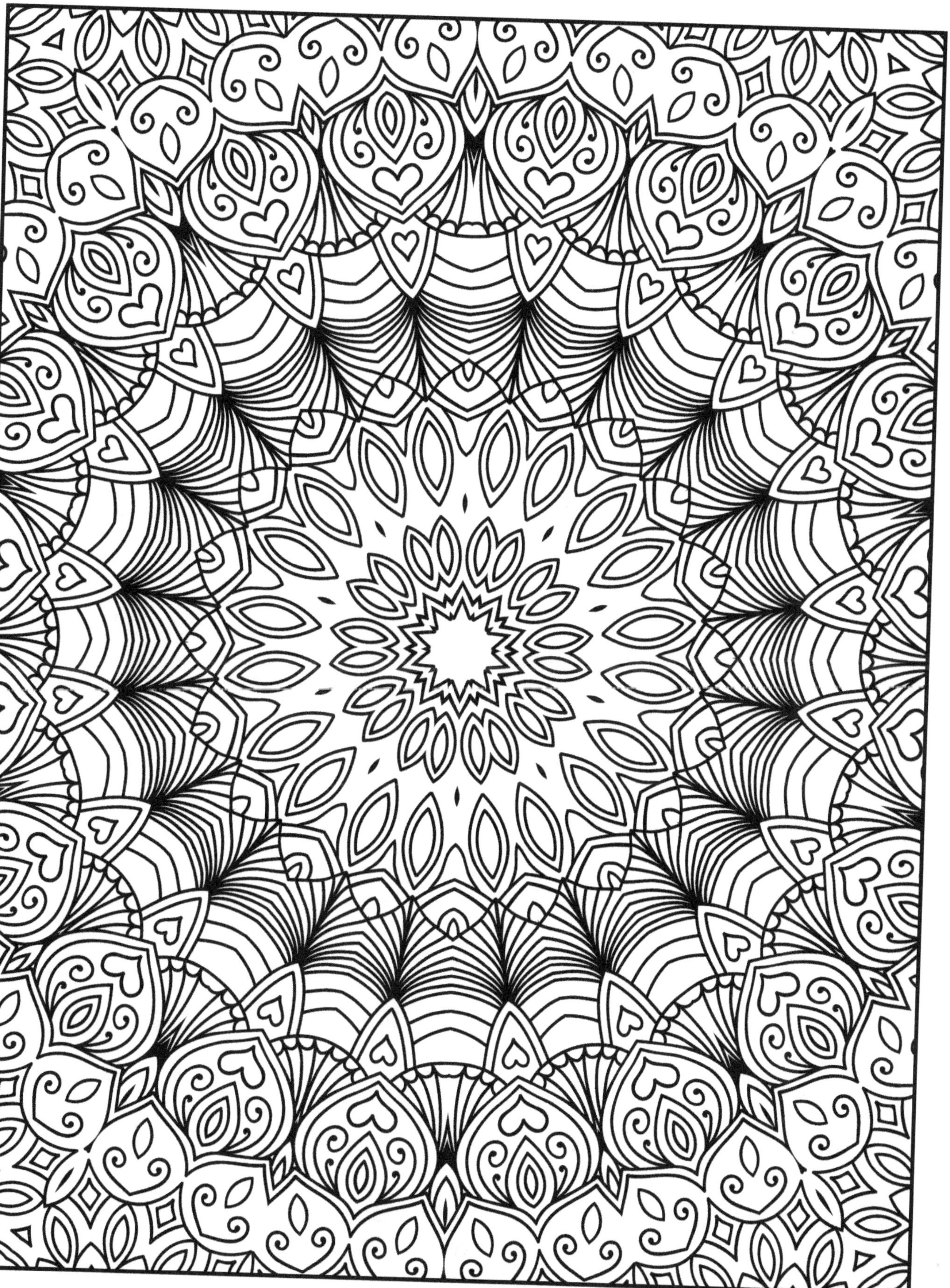

Fiction is like a spider's web, attached ever so slightly perhaps,
but still attached to life at all four corners.
Often the attachment is scarcely perceptible.
- Virginia Woolf

Be
An
Exceptional
Writer

Writing is its own reward.
– Henry Miller

Get it down.
Take chances.
It may be bad, but it's
the only way you
can do anything
really good.

William
Faulkner

I recognize terror as the finest emotion and so I will try to terrorize the reader.
But if I find that I cannot terrify, I will try to horrify, and if I find that
I cannot horrify, I'll go for the gross-out. I'm not proud.
- Stephen King

WRITE

The unread story is not a story; it is little black marks on wood pulp.
The reader, reading it, makes it live: a live thing, a story.
– Ursula K. Le Guin

You learn by writing short stories. Keep writing short stories. The money's in novels, but writing short stories keeps your writing lean and pointed.
– Larry Niven

DID YOU START A GREAT SHORT STORY YET?

What is wonderful about great literature is that it transforms the man
who reads it towards the condition of the man who wrote.
- E. M. Forster

Rejection slips, or form letters, however tactfully phrased, are lacerations of the soul, if not quite inventions of the devil—but there is no way around them.
 – Isaac Asimov

The most beautiful thing we can experience is the mysterious.
It is the source of all true art and science.
- Albert Einstein

All the world's a stage, and all the men and women merely players:
they have their exits and their entrances; and one man in his time
plays many parts, his acts being seven ages.
- William Shakespeare

Writing Prompts

Great is the art of beginning, but greater is the art of ending.
– Henry Wadsworth Longfellow

What are writing prompts?

Writing prompts are single paragraph, sometimes single sentence ideas that help you get past writer's block. It's an idea for a story that you can take and turn into a plot, fill it with characters and build a world around. They are starters, designed to grab your imagination and shake loose a story or two.

Need an idea to help get you started writing?

Here are some writing prompts for you:

July 2016 - You wake up one sunny day, go outside and look up. Instead of blue skies with fluffy clouds, you see thousands of flying saucers. After investigation by public officials, the media reports that we've been contacted by alien life. They have come, because Earth has just been made a stop in the galactic version of Pokemon Go.

What happens next?

❧❧

You go online to your local news site. You decide to check out recent crimes in your neighborhood. When you check the log, you find that your name is listed as having committed a crime. You have been mistakenly identified. As you read about yourself, there is a sudden loud knocking at your door followed by someone screaming, "It's the police. Open the door now."

What do you do? Do you open the door or jump out the window?

❧❧

Everyone has a superpower, and most make it public. People keep asking you what yours is, but you can't tell them - because if you tell them, they will kill themselves. The fact that you refuse to talk about it, it goes viral and you are eventually contacted by the news media. You're superpower makes you the harbinger of death. What happens when the press insists that you tell your superpower on national television where everyone who hears your power will commit suicide.

What do you do, and what's the result?

The best time to plan a book is while you're doing the dishes.
- Agatha Christie

No man has the right to dictate what other men should perceive, create or produce,
but all should be encouraged to reveal themselves, their perceptions and emotions,
and to build confidence in the creative spirit.
- Ansel Adams

Literature adds to reality, it does not simply describe it.
It enriches the necessary competencies that daily life requires and provides;
and in this respect, it irrigates the deserts that our lives have already become.
- C. S. Lewis

Writing Exercise

In Walt Whitman's own words, he explains the 10 Minute writing exercise. This is how he was so prolific in his writing career. He just went for it, and kept going capturing the heartbeat of life in his stories.

"The secret of it all, is to write in the gush, the throb, the flood, of the moment - tout things down without deliberation - without worrying about their style - without waiting for a fit time or place.

I always worked that way. I took the first scrap of paper, the first doorstep, the first desk, and wrote - wrote, wrote . . .

By writing at the instant the very heartbeat of life is caught."

- Walt Whitman

Here are four different objects. Start a story using all of them.

- A sleeping cat
- A pacing dog
- Two bent forks
- A potted plant

Write Like The Wind

Write for 10 minutes like before, and when you encounter the wall where you feel like you've run out of things to say, KEEP GOING. Keep going even if you have to write "garbage, garbage, garbage" until your Muse comes out. Your Muse will come in a whisper, a feeling or a continuation of scenes running in your mind's eye like a movie. Once you've gotten past the Wall, you will write like the wind, joyously and freely.

Start a story using these four things.

A sleeping cat • A pacing dog • Two bent forks • A potted plant

Why we write . . .
Literature is my Utopia. Here I am not disenfranchised.
No barrier of the senses shuts me out from the sweet,
gracious discourses of my book friends.
They talk to me without embarrassment or awkwardness.
- Helen Keller

What is Descriptionari?

Descriptionari is a writer's dream. It is a selection of descriptions of a wide variety of things including: love, hate, anger, passion, friendship, evil, gloom, pain -- the list goes on and on. Right now, there are **12,376 quotes, descriptions and writing prompts, 2,310 themes** in a database that is constantly expanding. If you're looking for a way to say your character is an inhuman monster, you will find lots of examples at Descriptionari for inspiration. You can take the provided descriptions and use them to write your own descriptions.

Here are some examples:

LOVE by Daisy

"Love, dearest Clementine, is not a spoken language at all, so listen not to tongues of silver. Love is in kind deeds, thoughtful actions, truthfulness, trustworthiness and self-sacrifice. Within that definition of love lies true passion, not at all the same thing as lust - a transitory satisfaction for the 'hungry ghost' soul. Know this, sweet child, and you'll have more love than your heart can hold even in the 'slim' years."

"Like my father before me, I am a force of nature, born to love like a hurricane - to rip out what is rotten so that new growth has a solid footing."

HATE by Daisy

I wasn't a hero until you came after my baby girl. Then it was war. You crossed the line and I don't forget. I won't rest until you're beaten - and I don't mean just beaten down. I mean dead. There isn't a place you can hide, I will find you, destroy you. I don't much care how it happens, I don't need you to suffer, I just need your cold black eyes extinguished from this universe. You may think it an overreaction, but you underestimated how much I love her. Don't think I'll play by "the rules" either, love allows us to exterminate vermin that attack children. I'm coming. Just know it.

HATE by Daisy

Donald spoke with a coldness she'd never heard before. "I don't just want to kill you, I want to put you in a pit and add the shovels of dirt slowly until your God damn mouth is full of muck. I want to hear your cries as the rocks rain down on you thicker than a hail storm. I don't care if you're sorry anymore, I don't want to hear it. You should have told me all that crap back when it could have made a difference, back when I loved you so much I would have gladly died in your place. You took what was beautiful in me and made it into what it is today. I hope you're proud, it's all your handiwork." He grinned showing yellowed teeth amongst the stubble, his eyes wider than any sane person's should be. Then he ran a hand through his thinning hair and pulled out the knife she'd bought him for their tenth anniversary in Rome.

A few more examples of descriptions from Descriptionari.com

Laughter by Azandtheunicorns

You could hear her sweet, joyful laughter from a mile away, it would echo through the halls and into each and every room in the house, and would cheer everyone up, it was at times like this that I liked having a 4 year old sister.

Smiles by James

When my baby smiles she lights up the room, everyone knows that. But what they can't see is that she lights me up inside so completely that my darkness disappears. She makes me whole and happy.

Fake Smile by Aisha

Ellis stared into Cecilia's eyes, determined not to look away first. He was certain that she knew he was trying to hide something, but still he was determined to fool her. He contorted his lips into an awkward, toothy smile, his but his cheeks were not so compromising. He could feel their reluctance to be moulded falsely. When Cecilia finally averted her gazed his smile fell lifeless, allowing his face to return to its usual cold hard gawk.

Used Car Salesman by Angela

Winds the clock back on the cars with an electric drill, hair slicked back, easy smile, twinkling eyes, charming, deceptive, greedy, dishonest, teeth as white as the driven snow, lies fluently, persuasive, laughs at any jokes the customer says whether they are funny or not, pays compliments, oily, slick, buttery voice, sharp suit, finds out how much money the customer has with sly questions, friendly, thinks customers are gullible suckers.

Giggles by Daisy

Ava's giggle softened the room, as if her gentle sound could make the lamplight more golden and the fires burn warmer.

Her giggle was a stone bouncing across a glossy lake, creating ripples of mirth where there had been none.

This is just a sampling. It a place with tons of descriptions, and you can use them as inspiration, and join and contribute your own descriptions to the mix.

I obviously have a knack for getting on paper what a lot of
people have thought and didn't realize they thought.
And they say, 'Hey, yeah!' And they like that.
- Andy Rooney

Do the one thing you think you cannot do. Fail at it. Try again.
Do better the second time. The only people who never tumble
are those who never mount the high wire.
- Oprah Winfrey

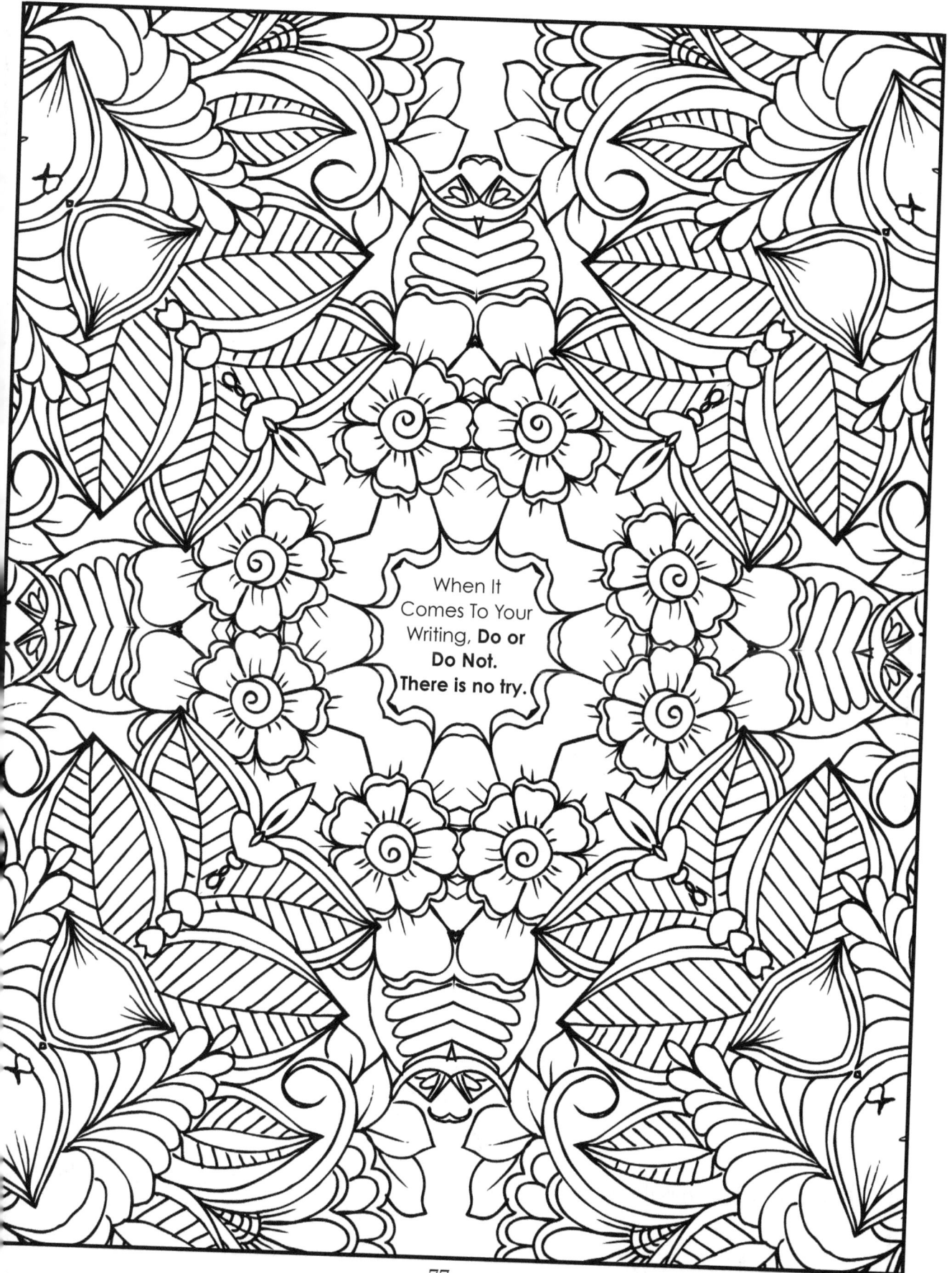

When It
Comes To Your
Writing, **Do or
Do Not.
There is no try.**

If science fiction is the mythology of modern technology, then its myth is tragic.
- Ursula K. LeGuin

Two Paragraph Story Ideas

Another secret weapon in my writing arsenal is Fiction Plots, Non-Fiction bullets- Bill Platt runs Fiction Plots, a great site if you're looking for plots for your stories and novels. In addition, he has a service and book based around two paragraph story ideas. Like writing prompts, the story ideas are jump starters to great fiction. If you're looking for a place to start, you might want to head on over to fictionplots.com. It's a membership site, and the value of the site far exceeds the modest monthly fee.

The only negative about this site is its navigation. You can tell the site was set up by a writer/artist and not a tech nerd. However, once you get the hang of it, it's easy to find what you need.

The two paragraph story ideas come in the following categories:
- Fantasy
- Mystery
- Romance
- Science Fiction
- Suspense

Here are a couple of examples of the stories. And yes, I realize that some of them are more than two paragraphs. LOL!

A Breath of Fresh Air

For as long as he could remember, they fought about everything under the sun. Money, what to make for dinner, the kids and the schools they were enrolled in and their various in-laws. Nothing was left out of their shouting matches. And yet, they did not wish to leave each other. It was like their fights kept them together. They fed off of each other's unhappiness and somehow that led to them staying in their situation.

When he finally moved out, he had decided long ago that he would never be like his parents. He was sick of the fighting. Now any time he heard an argument he got a sick feeling in his stomach and a pounding in his head.

She was like a breath of fresh air in the otherwise hellish world. She also had a little boy in need of a better father than the one occupying a jail cell, for thinking he could bully his girlfriend.

A Dark Past

She would not forget that strange man any time soon. He had been running from something though he said she had it all wrong. She knew that wasn't true. People don't go around looking over their shoulders, if they have a pleasant past. They had started up pleasant conversations there in that bed and breakfast. Her parents ran the place and she worked for them during the summer when she came home from college.

He had booked a room there for three nights before he said he had to move on. Every morning he would invite her to sit and talk with him after her shift was done. He would stare into his mug of coffee with both hands wrapped around the hot ceramic and just talk about some of the things he enjoyed. Most of the time they talked of her.

A Litter of Kittens

He saw her for the first time in the alley behind the restaurant where he worked.

She was nursing one of the abandoned baby kittens from a tiny bottle while the rest scrambled at her feet, squealing for their turn. She let him help her, her wary demeanor vanishing when she noticed how gently he handled the babies.

She explained that she was a veterinary student and that she would have taken all the kittens in if she did not have roommates who were allergic.

He had only one roommate who was barely there, and so he volunteered to be the one to give them a home. That way she could see the kittens whenever she wanted and he could see her often.

When he left, she had been saddened. She had felt something between them, a connection she couldn't explain. She was washing tables and thinking of him when the bell rang, signaling a customer. She looked up into a familiar pair of pale green eyes.

Europa's Embrace

NASA is overjoyed when they have a successful mission to Europa, one of Jupiter's moons. The astronauts have brought back samples of water from there to test for the potential of harvesting the water for people who have little access to fresh water.

When a sample of the water disappears from the lab and is dumped into the Atlantic Ocean, ice crystals begin to form as particles within react with the water on earth. Millions of marine life are wiped out due to the freezing waters and soon, the entire ocean will be frozen over if nothing can be done to stop the reaction.

Amnesia Is Only The Beginning

When he wakes in the hospital and finds that he has no memories of what has happened in the last two days, he turns to find answers from the only person in the room: the man who has been sitting beside him for as long as he's been admitted. The man explains that he is a bodyguard, sent by a powerful client who employed the patient before his unfortunate accident. When he asks what he was doing, the man just smiles at him.

His memories come back slowly and when they do, that is when the encore of unwanted visitors begins. Each time someone enters who is not part of the hospital staff, the bulky bodyguard takes them out and throws their lifeless bodies out the window. He may not have the stomach to see what happens to those bodies after the bull of a man is done with them.

I've gotten a lot of good stories and plots from Fiction Plots, and these two paragraph (or thereabouts) story starters are an invaluable addition to my writing arsenal. He also has another site that non-fiction writers would love called NF Bullets which is all kinds of research for non-fiction blog posts and articles. It's located at NFBullets.com.

Writer's Resources

Need some writer's prompts?

Here's some places I've used:

Writing Prompts

Reddit
reddit.gofindoutmore.com

Writer's Digest
wd.gofindoutmore.com

Building Your Characters

The Epic Guide Character Chart for Fiction Writers
Printable character building form
epiguide.gofindoutmore.com

Helpers & Inspiration

Database of Descriptions for Inspiration
12,376 quotes, descriptions and writing prompts
desc.gofindoutmore.com

Plots & Story Starters

Bill Platt's Fiction Plots & Two Paragraph Story Starters
fictionplots.gofindoutmore.com

Bill Platts Non-Fiction Bullets
Ideas for non-fiction blog posts and articles
nfbullets.gofindoutmore.com

He also put out an ebook called Fiction Story Prompts. You can find it here:
50prompts.gofindoutmore.com

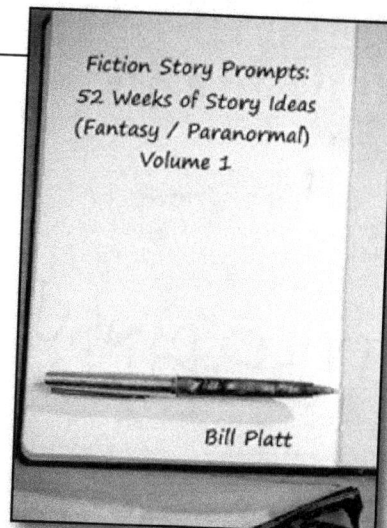

Fiction Story Prompts:
52 Weeks of Story Ideas
(Fantasy / Paranormal)
Volume 1

Bill Platt

Excellent Writer's List Guides

It goes without saying that if you're a writer, you should have some basic tools in your arsenal: dictionary, thesaurus, Strunk & White, etc. In addition, a nice set of guides to invest in are the lists books. One set of lists books covers a wide variety of things in wriing:

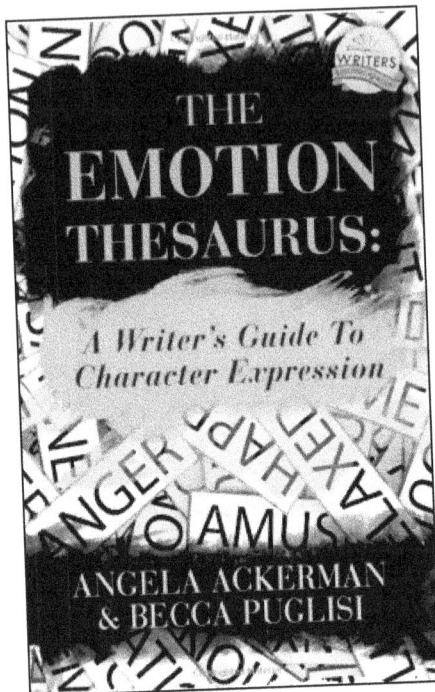

The Emotion Thesaurus:
A Writer's Guide to Character Expression

One of the biggest problem areas for writers is conveying a character's emotions to the reader in a unique, compelling way. This book comes to the rescue by highlighting 75 emotions and listing the possible body language cues, thoughts, and visceral responses for each.

Using its easy-to-navigate list format, readers can draw inspiration from character cues that range in intensity to match any emotional moment. The Emotion Thesaurus also tackles common emotion-related writing problems and provides methods to overcome them. This writing tool encourages writers to show, not tell emotion and is a creative brainstorming resource for any fiction project.

For more info, go to: emotion.gofindoutmore.com

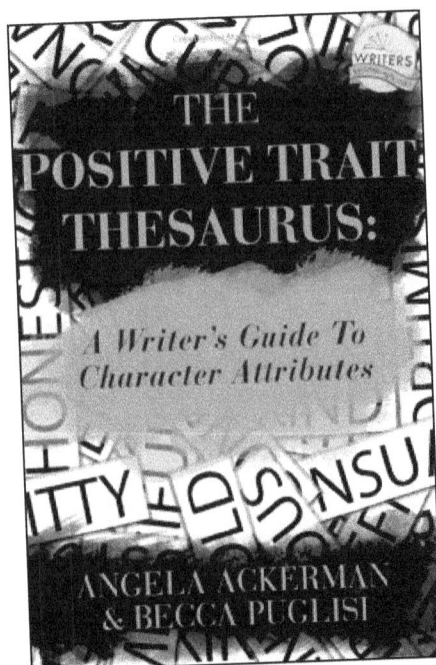

The Positive Trait Thesaurus
A Writer's Guide To Character Attributes

If you find character creation difficult or worry that your cast members all seem the same, The Positive Trait Thesaurus is brimming with ideas to help you develop one-of-a-kind, dynamic characters that readers will love. Extensively indexed, with entries written in a user-friendly list format, this brainstorming resource is perfect for any character creation project.

A large selection of attributes to choose from when building a personality profile. Each entry lists possible causes for why a trait might emerge, along with associated attitudes, behaviors, thoughts, and emotions. There are also downloadable tools for organizing a character's attributes.

For more info, go to: positive.gofindoutmore.com

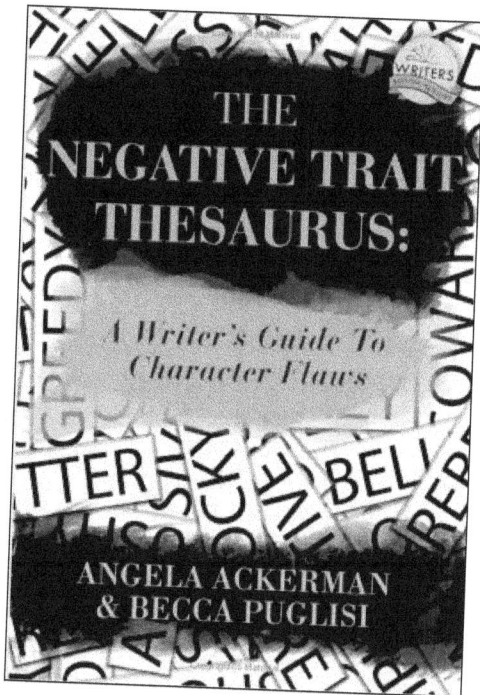

The Positive Trait Thesaurus
A Writer's Guide To Character Attributes

Crafting likable, interesting characters is a balancing act, and finding that perfect mix of strengths and weaknesses can be difficult. But the task has become easier thanks to The Negative Trait Thesaurus.

Through its flaw-centric exploration of character arc, motivation, emotional wounds, and basic needs, writers will learn which flaws make the most sense for their heroes, villains, and other members of the story's cast. Inside The Negative Trait Thesaurus you'll find a vast collection of flaws to explore when building a character's personality. Each entry includes possible causes, attitudes, behaviors, thoughts, and related emotions.

For more info, go to: emotion.gofindoutmore.com

Strunk & White
The Elements of Style

When I write, whether it is a blog post, short story or novel, I use a handful of reference tools: a dictionary, thesaurus, the guides listed previously, Writer's Market and Strunk & White's, Elements of Style. The Elements of Style is a incredible, extraordinarily concise, wonderfully-written tool that puts the polish on any piece of writing.

It begins with eleven "Elementary Rules of Usage," and continues with "Elementary Rules of Composition," and eleven "Matters of Form." It's presented in a to-the-point style that gives a couple lines of explanation with a couple of examples. The compilation is only thirty-eight pages long, but it covers 90% of writing fundamentals.

Chapter IV there is a twenty-seven page, alphabetical listing of commonly misused words and expressions. This section alone is worth the price of the book. What I do is take my completed manuscript and use this chapter to check via my word processor. Problematic words and phrases are exposed and can be fixed.

This is just a sampling of this classic book that has stood the test of time. It is as relevant and useful today as when it was originally published in 1918. If you're serious about writing, this book should be on your bookshelf.

For more info, go to: strunk.gofindoutmore.com

Notes, Doodles & Ruminations

Notes, Doodles & Ruminations

Notes, Doodles & Ruminations

Notes, Doodles & Ruminations

ABOUT THE AUTHOR

Maya Sheppard was born and raised in Philadelphia, Pennsylvania. As a cancer survivor, single mother and lover of books, she found grounding in her faith and escape through writing and cooking and recently, adult coloring books. Mother to one exceptional daughter and four rescue cats, Maya finds every day an adventure and every breath she takes a blessing from above. She wants to share her passions and interests with other readers, and hope that you enjoy her work.

Be sure and check out her other adult coloring book,

COLOR ME COOKBOOK

Find out more here: colormecookbook.gofindoutmore.com

www.ingramcontent.com/pod-product-compliance
Lightning Source LLC
Chambersburg PA
CBHW081220020426

42331CB00012B/3054